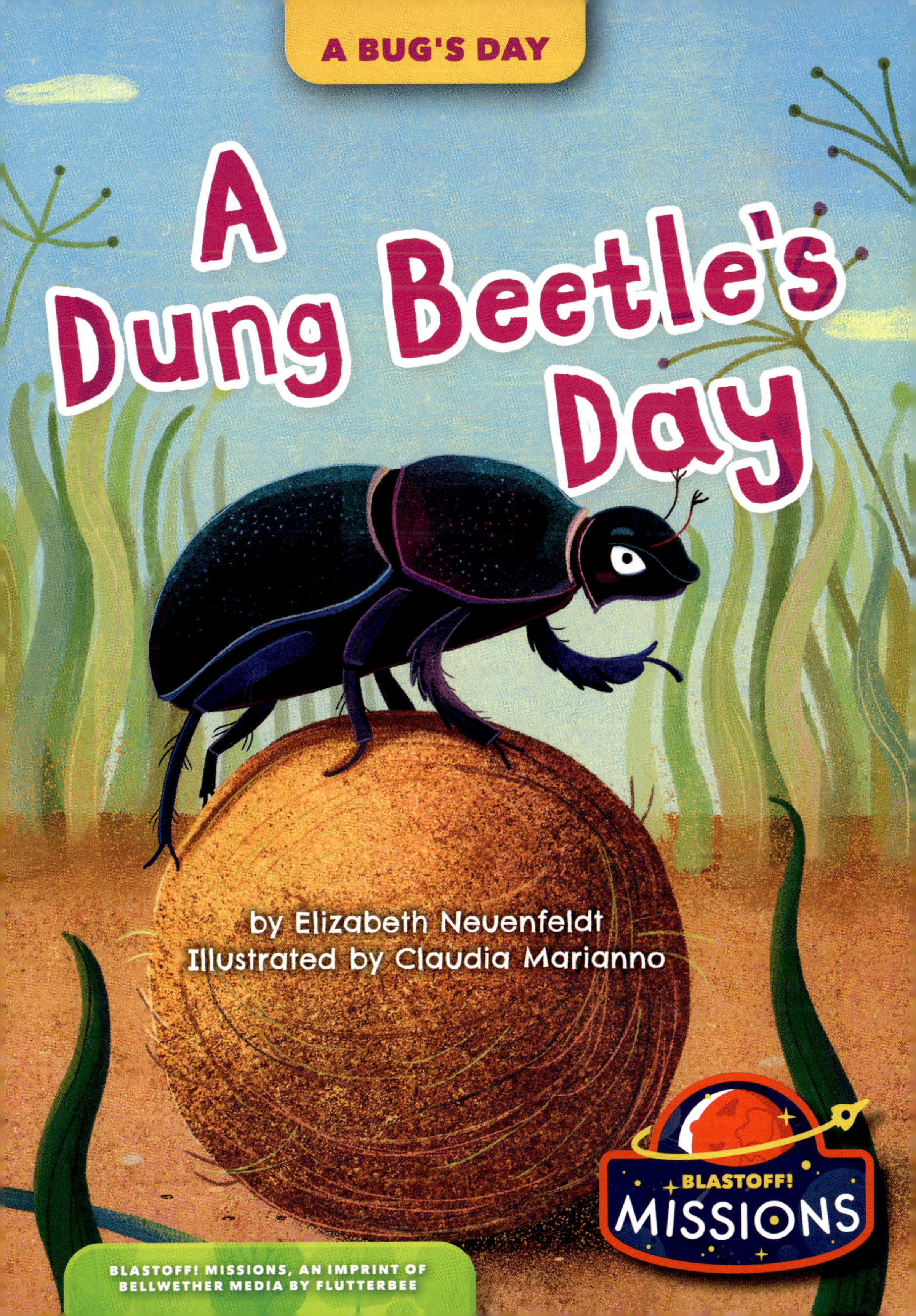
A BUG'S DAY
A Dung Beetle's Day
by Elizabeth Neuenfeldt
Illustrated by Claudia Marianno
BLASTOFF! MISSIONS
BLASTOFF! MISSIONS, AN IMPRINT OF BELLWETHER MEDIA BY FLUTTERBEE

Blastoff! Missions takes you on a learning adventure! Colorful illustrations and exciting narratives highlight cool facts about our world and beyond. Read the mission goals and follow the narrative to gain knowledge, build reading skills, and have fun!

Traditional Nonfiction

Narrative Nonfiction

Blastoff! Universe

MISSION GOALS

- FIND YOUR SIGHT WORDS IN THE BOOK.
- LEARN WHAT A DUNG BEETLE DOES IN A DAY.
- LEARN HOW A DUNG BEETLE USES DUNG.

This edition first published in 2027 by Bellwether Media, Inc.

For information regarding permission, write to Bellwether Media, Inc., Attention: Permissions Department, 3500 American Blvd W, Suite 150, Bloomington, MN 55431.

Library of Congress Cataloging-in-Publication Data

Names: Neuenfeldt, Elizabeth author | Marianno, Claudia, illustrator. Title: A dung beetle's day / by Elizabeth Neuenfeldt; illustrated by Claudia Marianno.
Description: Minneapolis, Minnesota : Bellwether Media, Inc, [2027] | Series: A bug's day | Includes bibliographical references and index. | Audience: Ages 5-8 | Audience: Grades 2-3 | Summary: "Vibrant illustrations accompany information about dung beetles. The narrative nonfiction text is intended for students in kindergarten through third grade."-- Provided by publisher.
Identifiers: LCCN 2026001562 (print) | LCCN 2026001563 (ebook) | ISBN 9798898800871 (library binding) | ISBN 9798898802110 (ebook)
Subjects: LCSH: Dung beetles--Behavior--Juvenile literature | Dung beetles--Juvenile literature | Insects--Juvenile literature
Classification: LCC QL596.S3 N48 2027 (print) | LCC QL596.S3 (ebook)
LC record available at https://lccn.loc.gov/2026001562
LC ebook record available at https://lccn.loc.gov/2026001563

Editor: Betsy Rathburn Designer: Laura Sowers

Printed in the United States of America, North Mankato, MN.

This is **Blastoff Jimmy**! He is here to help you on your mission and share fun facts along the way!

Table of Contents

Dung Day

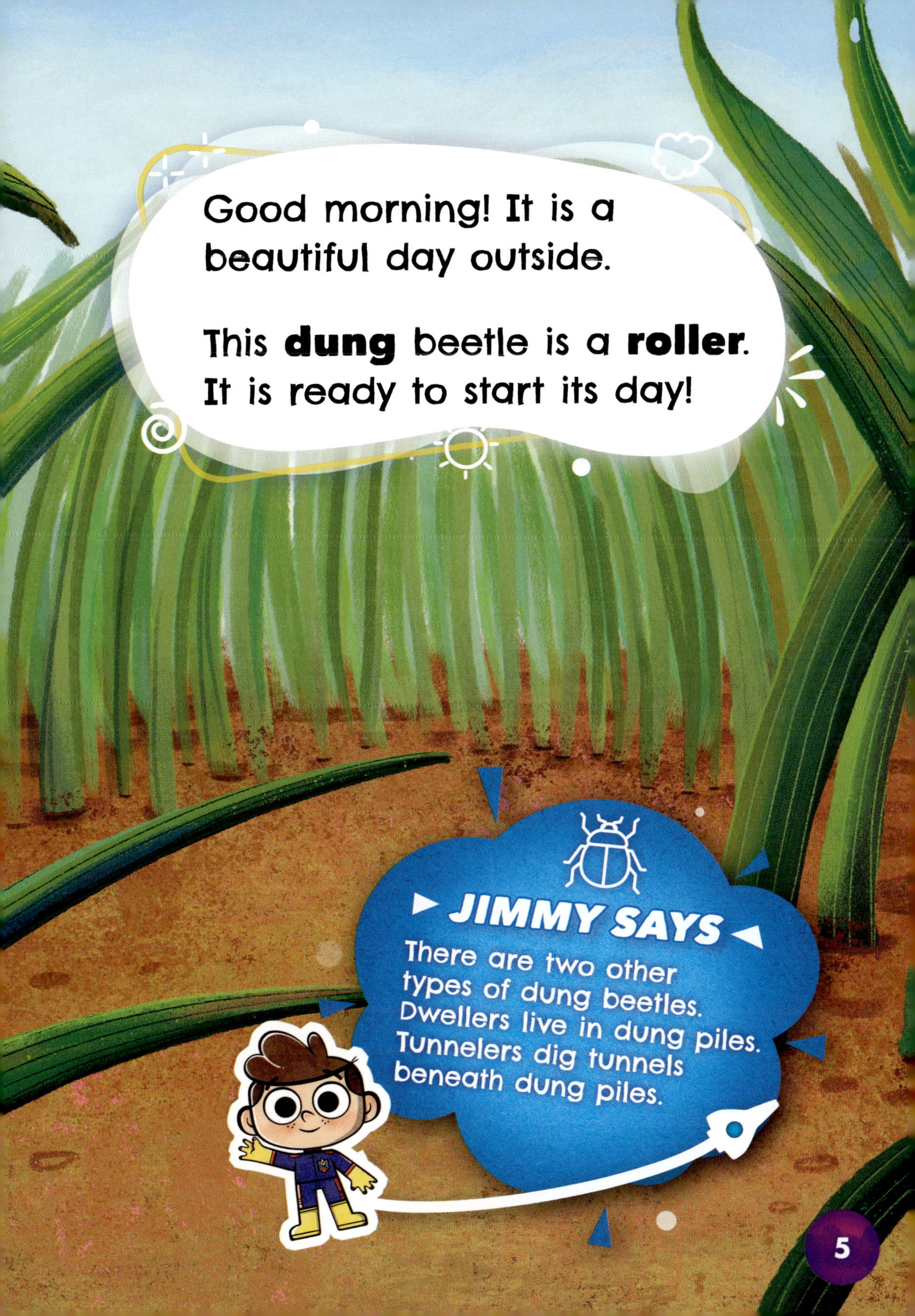

Good morning! It is a beautiful day outside.

This **dung** beetle is a **roller**. It is ready to start its day!

JIMMY SAYS

There are two other types of dung beetles. Dwellers live in dung piles. Tunnelers dig tunnels beneath dung piles.

The dung beetle walks through a field. It senses its surroundings with its **antennae**.

It feels a **vibration**.
A **predator** is nearby. Hide!

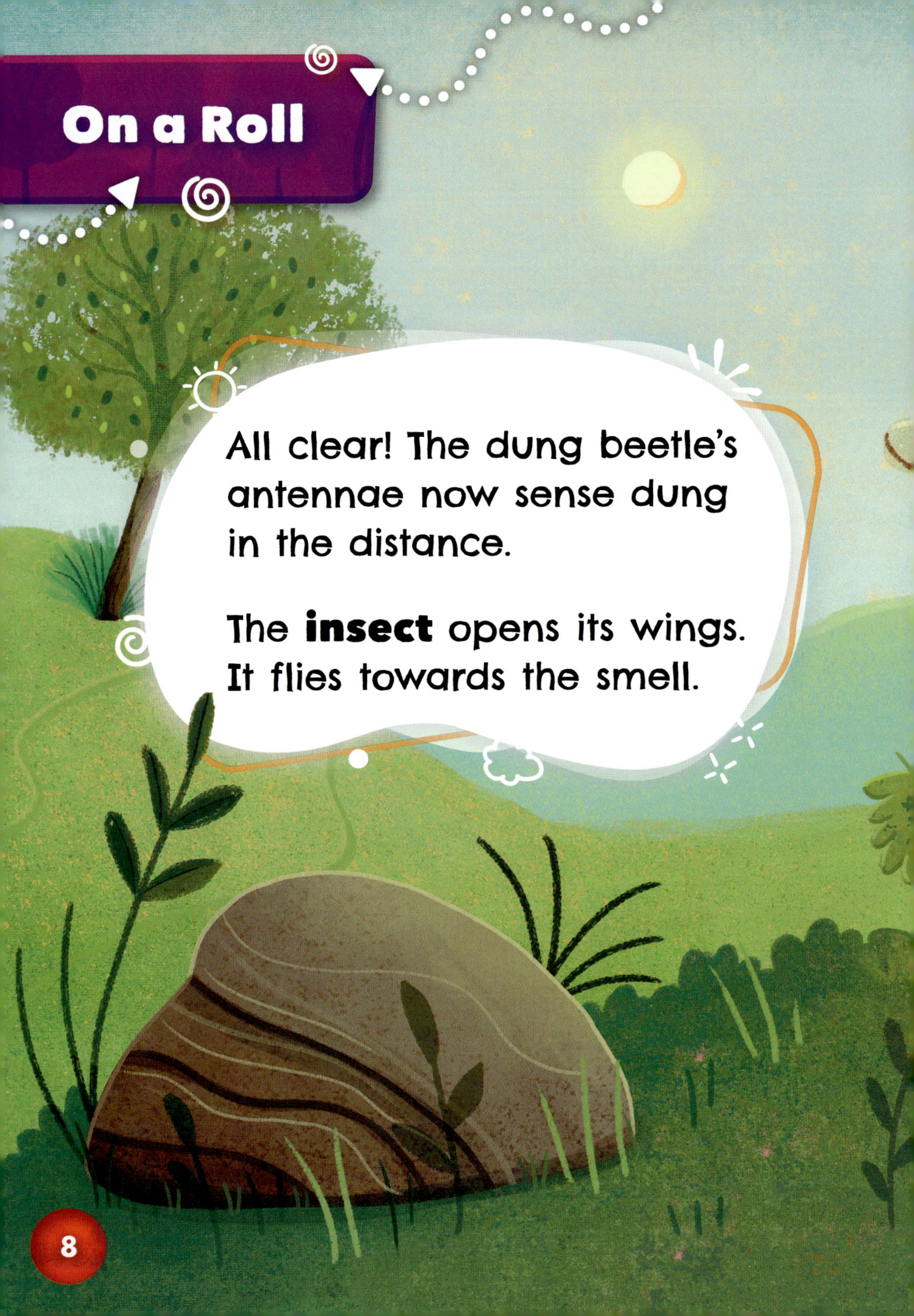

On a Roll

All clear! The dung beetle's antennae now sense dung in the distance.

The **insect** opens its wings. It flies towards the smell.

The dung beetle lands on a nearby dung pile. It gathers pieces of dung.

It uses its legs to pack the pieces together. It makes a round ball of dung!

Here comes another dung beetle. It is trying to steal the ball of dung!

The dung beetles fight with their strong front legs.

We have a winner! The dung beetle rolls the ball in a straight line. The ball is big. But the beetle is strong!

Next, the beetle finds a **mate**.

mate

young
dung beetle

JIMMY SAYS

Some dung beetles can pull up to 1,141 times their body weight!

The dung beetle buries an egg inside the dung ball.

Soon the egg **hatches**. A young dung beetle eats from the dung ball.

Time to Eat

The adult dung beetle flies back to the dung pile. It makes another ball of dung.

This one is food.

The dung beetle buries the dung ball. This **aerates** the soil. It keeps the soil healthy!

This beetle had a **productive** day!

All About Dung Beetles

Body Parts

Things Seen

dung

predator

young

Glossary

aerates–exposes to the air

antennae–feelers connected to a dung beetle's head that sense information around them

dung–poop

hatches–breaks open

insect–a small animal with six legs and a hard outer body; an insect's body is divided into three parts.

mate–a partner

predator–an animal that hunts other animals for food

productive–giving results

roller–a dung beetle that rolls dung away from a dung pile and buries it in the ground

vibration–a movement caused by something moving quickly back and forth

To Learn More

AT THE LIBRARY

Alderman, Alice. *Small Mighty Dung Beetle.* Brooklyn, N.Y.: Red Comet Press, 2025.

Chanez, Katie. *Gross Animal Eaters.* Minneapolis, Minn.: Jump!, 2025.

Murray, Julie. *Beetles.* Minneapolis, Minn.: Abdo Zoom, 2022.

ON THE WEB

FACTSURFER

Factsurfer.com gives you a safe, fun way to find more information.

1. Go to www.factsurfer.com.

2. Enter "a dung beetle's day" into the search box and click 🔍.

3. Select your book cover to see a list of related content.

BEYOND THE MISSION

> WHAT FACT FROM THE BOOK DID YOU THINK WAS THE MOST INTERESTING?

> DRAW A DUNG BEETLE. WHICH BODY PARTS DO YOU THINK ARE MOST IMPORTANT?

> WHAT ARE SOME ACTIVITIES THAT YOU DO EVERY DAY?

Index